At Home with Science

Counting Sheep!

Why do we sleep?

Written by Janice Lobb

Illustrated by Peter Utton and Ann Savage

KINGFISHER

KINGFISHER
Kingfisher Publications Plc
New Penderel House
283-288 High Holborn
London WC1V 7HZ
www.kingfisherpub.com

First published by Kingfisher Publications Plc 2001
10 9 8 7 6 5 4 3 2 1

1TR/0501/FR/SC/128JDA

Created and designed by Snapdragon Publishing Ltd
Copyright © Snapdragon Publishing Ltd 2001

ISBN 0 7534 0559 8

Printed in Hong Kong/China

Author Janice Lobb
Illustrators Peter Utton and Ann Savage

For Snapdragon
Editorial Director Jackie Fortey
Art Director Chris Legee
Designers Chris Legee and Joy Fitzsimons

For Kingfisher
Editors Jennie Morris and Emma Wild
Series Art Editor Mike Davis
DTP Co-ordinator Nicky Studdart
Production Debbie Otter

Contents

About this book

Have you ever asked why you have to go to bed, or how the Moon gets its light, or wondered why your hair sometimes stands on end when you brush it? This book is about the science that is happening every day, in your bedroom. Look around and you'll soon be making your own discoveries!

What if?

Why?

Where?

Which?

How?

Hall of Fame

Archie and his friends are here to help you. They are each named after a famous scientist – apart from Bob the duck, who is a young scientist just like you!

Archie

ARCHIMEDES (287–212BC) The Greek scientist Archimedes worked out why things float or sink while in the bath. According to the story, he was so pleased that he leapt out, shouting 'Eureka!' which means 'I've done it!'

Frank

BENJAMIN FRANKLIN (1706–1790) This American statesman carried out a famous (but dangerous) experiment in 1752. By flying a kite in a storm, he showed that a flash of lightning was electricity. This helped people to protect buildings during storms.

Marie

MARIE CURIE (1867–1934) Girls did not go to university in Poland, where Marie Curie grew up, so she went to study in Paris, France. She worked on radioactivity and received two Nobel prizes for her discoveries, in 1903 and 1911.

Dot

DOROTHY HODGKIN (1910–1994) Dorothy Hodgkin was a British scientist who made many important discoveries about molecules and atoms, the tiny particles that make up everything around us. She was given the Nobel prize for Chemistry in 1964.

See for yourself!

1 Read about the science in your bedroom, then try the 'See for yourself!' experiments to discover how it works. In science, experiments try to find or show the answers.

Ooooo!

Tu-whit Tu-whoo!

2 Read the instructions for each experiment carefully, making sure you follow the numbered steps in the correct order.

Crunch!

Twang!

3 Here are some of the things you will need. Have everything ready before you start each experiment.

Fabric scraps

Double-sided tape

Plastic bottle

Jam jar lids

Plastic straws

Spoon

Ball

Silver ball

Scissors

Essential oils

Mug

Thread

Drawing pins

Button

Silver coin

4 ## Safety first! ✋

Some scientists took risks to make their discoveries, but our experiments are safe. Just make sure that you tell an adult what you are doing, and get their help when you see the red warning button.

Amazing facts

WOW!

You'll notice that some words are written in *italics*. You can learn more about them from the glossary at the back of the book. And if you want to find out some amazing facts, look out for the 'Wow!' panels.

Look out for the useful tips!

Have fun!

Why do I need to go to bed?

When you are awake, your brain – the part of your body which controls what you do – receives information from your *senses*. They tell it about everything you see, hear, taste, smell and feel. Your brain needs time to sort this out, which it does when you are asleep. Dreaming is part of the sorting process. The brain stores most memories, but lets you forget things which you don't need. If you don't get enough sleep, you can become muddled, or even ill.

> When is the best time to go to bed?

> When the bed won't come to you!

Sweet dreams!

There are things that you do all the time without thinking, such as breathing. This happens even while you are asleep. Part of your brain keeps you alive without you having to think about it.

Your heart carries on beating when you are asleep.

Dream

Brain

Even when you are asleep, your brain sends messages to your breathing muscles.

Children grow more when they are asleep than when they are awake.

Plenty of 'beauty sleep' gives your skin a chance to repair itself.

Sleeping when you are ill helps you to recover.

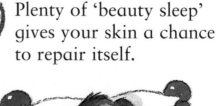

See for yourself!

1 Try to learn a rhyme before you go to bed. Can you remember it the next morning?

2 Try to learn another rhyme when you get up. Can you remember it when you go to bed? What is the best time to learn new things?

3 If you remember your dreams when you wake up, try to write them down. You will usually forget them quickly if you don't.

In his dream, Archie is dancing with Bob. What do you dream about?

Sleeping beauty

WOW!

On average, a person spends 23 years of their life asleep, but not usually all at once!

Try to sleep at the right times!

Why do I have bedding?

The coverings, pillows and mattress on your bed help to make you comfy while you sleep. If the air around you is cold, you lose *heat* by *convection*. This means that, as the air next to your body warms up and moves away, it takes heat with it. Your duvet or blanket stops this from happening by acting as *insulation*. The warm air is trapped and cannot escape. In hot weather, when you are already warm, you will probably need thinner sheets.

It hasn't been made yet!

Shall I tell you the joke about the bed?

Saving heat

Animals and birds have thick fur and feathers, or make nests of insulating materials to keep their babies warm.

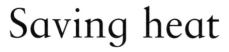

Feather-filled duvet

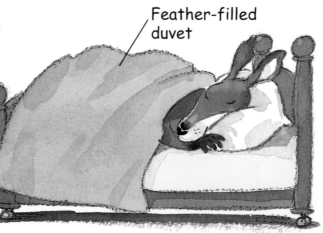

We use similar materials in duvets and blankets to trap warm air and keep it close to our bodies. Mattresses are softer and warmer than the cold, hard ground.

Insulation can keep heat out as well as in. Picnic food will stay cool in a padded bag.

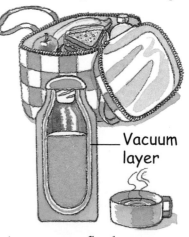

Vacuum layer

A *vacuum* flask can keep drinks hot or cold.

See for yourself! ✋

1 Collect scraps of different fabric, such as a cotton tea towel, a woolly jumper, a silk scarf, and furry material.

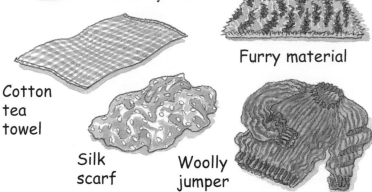

Furry material

Cotton tea towel

Silk scarf

Woolly jumper

2 Now see how well they act as insulation. Ask a grown-up to fill some plastic drinks bottles with hand-hot water.

Caps on

3 Wrap each bottle, except for one, in a piece of material. Leave them to cool in the same place.

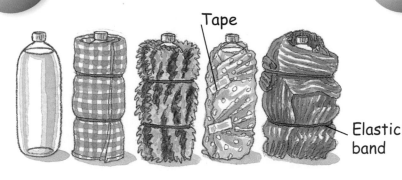

Tape

Elastic band

4 After about 30 minutes, feel the bottles. Are any of them still hot? Put them in order. Which material was the best insulator?

Which material would make the best cover for Archie's hot-water bottle?

WOW!

Hair

Llama

Hollow hairs

Most mammals and birds have air trapped between their hair or feathers to help them keep warm. Llamas go one better and have hollow hairs which give them extra insulation.

Don't forget to make your bed!

9

Why does my clock tick?

Your bedroom clock may make a loud ticking noise, but it helps you to get up every day. It works day and night, showing hours and minutes. Long ago, people got up when the Sun rose, and measured hours using silent sand timers. Ticking clocks have moving parts called 'clockwork'. Clockwork is when gearwheels are turned by *energy* stored in a battery or wound-up spring. The clock 'ticks' as the gearwheels click round. The clock stops ticking when the battery or spring runs down.

What do you do with a sick clock?

Nothing, it will get better in time!

How clocks work

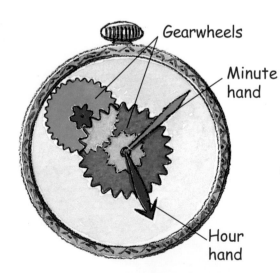

Gearwheels

Minute hand

Hour hand

The gearwheels inside a clock turn the big (minute) hand and the little (hour) hand at different speeds, so we can tell the time.

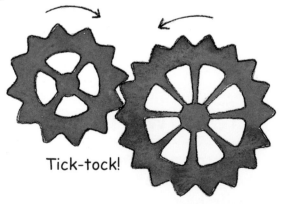

One wheel goes one way, and the other goes the opposite way.

Tick-tock!

A gearwheel is a wheel with teeth round the edge. The teeth on one wheel catch on the next and help it turn round.

Instead of a face and hands, a *digital* clock has a *liquid crystal display* (LCD) which just shows numbers.

Clockwork clock

Digital clock

10

See for yourself! ✋

1 To make a gearwheel, cut up some plastic straws carefully. Use double-sided tape to stick ten of the pieces to the top of a large jam jar lid.

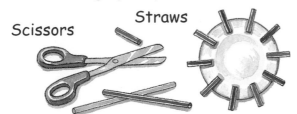

Scissors   Straws

2 Using a smaller lid, make another gearwheel with eight teeth. These are your model gearwheels.

Eight teeth

Ten teeth

3 Ask a grown-up to stick a drawing pin in the middle of the underside of each gearwheel. This will help your gearwheels to turn.

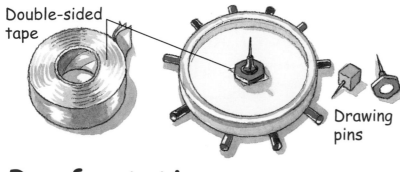

Double-sided tape

Drawing pins

4 Push the drawing pins into a cardboard box, so that when the gearwheels turn, the teeth catch on each other. Turn the big wheel and watch it turn the little wheel.

Perfect time

WOW!

The most accurate clock is an atomic clock, which loses less than one second in three million years. A quartz crystal, like the ones in digital watches, is made to *vibrate* using a special metal called caesium. One second is the time taken for 9,192,631,770 vibrations, which is very fast indeed.

Practise telling the right time!

Why does my hair stand on end?

What did the brush say to the hair?

I'm going to charge you!

Is it sometimes impossible to get your hair to lie flat when you brush it? Does it stand on end when you comb it? This problem is caused by *static electricity*. When you use a plastic brush or comb, you strip away tiny electrical *particles* called *electrons* from your hair. This leaves the outside of each hair *electrically charged*. Because the charges on each hair are the same, the electricity pushes the hairs away from each other, so they fluff out instead of lying flat together.

Electrical charges

Magnets will push each other away like electrically charged hairs. If you move the same ends, or *poles*, of two magnets together, they repel, or push, each other away. North (N) will repel north, and south (S) will repel south.

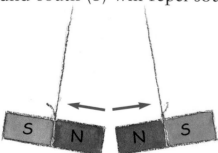

Do Not Disturb

Walking around on a thick carpet can charge your whole body. If you touch a metal door handle, you may get a surprise jolt from a little electric shock!

Static electricity can also attract objects. It attracts dust to glass windows and TV screens.

Charges that are different attract, or pull towards, each other.

See for yourself!

1 Mix some coarse salt or sugar with finely-ground pepper or talcum powder. Sprinkle the mixture on a flat surface.

2 Rub a plastic spoon or ruler with a woolly cloth, or the sleeve of your jumper, to charge it with static electricity.

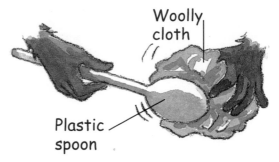

Woolly cloth

Plastic spoon

3 Hold the spoon over the mixture and gradually lower it. The fine powder or pepper will jump up to the spoon and stick to it.

Fine powder

4 If you lower the spoon further, some of the salt or sugar will jump up as well. Static electricity makes this happen.

Salt and sugar are heavier than fine powder.

Charged clouds

Electrical charges

WOW!

In thunderstorms, swirling ice particles in clouds rub together and become charged with static electricity. This produces lightning. Huge sparks of *electricity* jump through the air and can travel between clouds, or down to the ground.

Try sticking balloons to the wall using static!

How does my lamp work?

Why have you got a book about lamps?

For a little light reading!

When things become *white-hot*, they send out some of their energy as *light*. The energy in a candle comes from the burning wax. The candle gets shorter as the wax is used up. When you switch on an electric lamp, the bulb lights up. Unlike a candle, the bulb is not used up, because it does not burn. The energy it uses is electricity, which travels to the bulb through wires for as long as the lamp is switched on.

How light travels

Inside a glass light bulb there is a fine metal wire called the *filament*. When electricity flows through the filament, it becomes white-hot and gives out light.

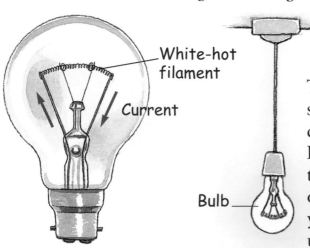

White-hot filament

Current

Bulb

The light is sent out in all directions. If you want it to go in only one direction, you must use a shade.

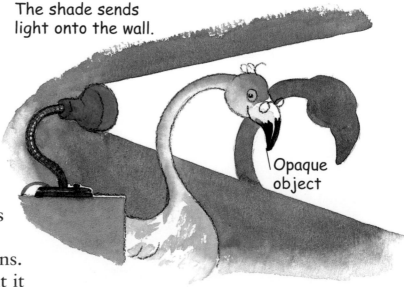

The shade sends light onto the wall.

Opaque object

Light always travels in straight lines, so it cannot go around corners. When light reaches an *opaque* object that blocks its way, it casts a shadow.

See for yourself! ✋ Bright idea!

1 Ask a grown-up to make a hole in two pieces of card. Hold up one piece at arm's length between you and a lamp. You can see the light shining through the hole.

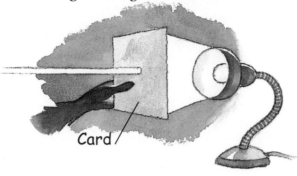

Card

2 Hold up the second piece of card between you and the first piece. You can only see the light if the two holes are lined up.

WOW!

Light

A famous US inventor, Thomas Edison, made the first electric light bulb in 1879. It contained a filament made of carbon, which glowed when an electric current passed through it. People soon began to replace gas lamps in their homes with electric lights.

3 Let the lamp shine on a wall. Use your hands or make a puppet to put between the lamp and the wall. Have some fun making shadow pictures.

Is this a butterfly or a bird?

Don't touch! It might still be hot!

What's in my wardrobe?

Humans wear clothes because, unlike other animals, we often need extra protection against the weather. When it is hot, lightweight clothes allow heat to escape from our skin and protect us from the Sun. Lighter colours, such as white, also *reflect* sunlight, and help to keep us cool. In cold weather, we wear warmer and heavier clothes that trap air and keep in heat. People who make clothes dye materials in many colours so that we can choose to wear our favourites, and look different from everyone else.

What do you call a cross between a sheep and a wallaby?

A woolly jumper!

Fibres and dyes

Clothes are made from *fibres*. Some fibres are natural. Cotton and linen are from plants, while wool and silk come from animals.

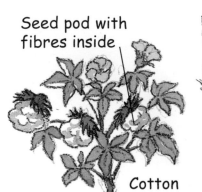

Seed pod with fibres inside

Cotton plant

Some fibres have several natural colours. Jacob sheep, for example, have several shades in their wool.

Wool

Jacob sheep

Liquid chemicals

Fibres

Liquid chemicals are squirted through holes in a machine, to make *synthetic* fibres.

Thread

Dye

Coal

Most of the *dyes* used to colour clothes are made from oil or coal. There are thousands of different colours to choose from.

See for yourself!

1 How many ways can you sort your clothes? Look at the care labels to help you decide. Which ones contain synthetic, fibres? Polyester, nylon and acrylic are examples of synthetic fibres.

2 Which clothes are for cold weather? If they trap air, because they are fluffy or padded, they keep in heat well. Thin clothes are better for warmer weather.

Fluffy jumper   Thin vest

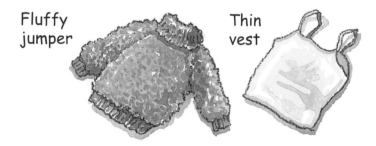

3 Do you have a favourite colour? If you sort your clothes into different colours, is there one pile which is larger than all the rest?

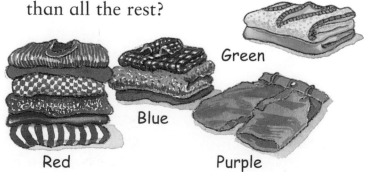

Red   Blue   Green   Purple

North Pole

Arctic hare with summer coat

Arctic hare with winter coat

WOW!

All change!

There are animals, such as the Arctic hare and the snow mouse, that have a different coat for each season. The Arctic hare is greyish-brown in summer, but in winter its coat turns white to blend in with the snow. This helps it to hide from its enemies. Near the North Pole, where there is always snow, it stays white throughout the year.

Keep your clothes tidy, or you will never find anything!

Why does perfume smell nice?

An elephant's trunk!

What's long, grey and smells?

We smell things when tiny particles drift through the air and up into our noses. Special scent detectors catch the particles and send messages to our brains. Our sense of smell helps us enjoy the food we eat. We also enjoy smells for their own sake, like the scents that many flowers use to attract insects. There are smelly chemicals in other parts of plants too. They are extracted from plants as *essential oils* and used to make perfumes.

How smells travel

Essential oils *evaporate* and are easy to smell. We cannot smell things, such as salt and metal, that don't turn into vapour.

Liquid scent turns into vapour. Vapour travels through the air.

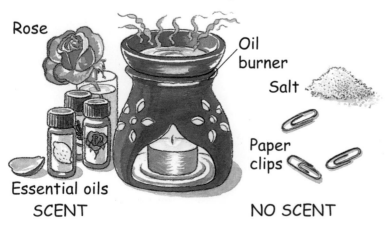

Rose

Oil burner

Salt

Paper clips

Essential oils
SCENT

NO SCENT

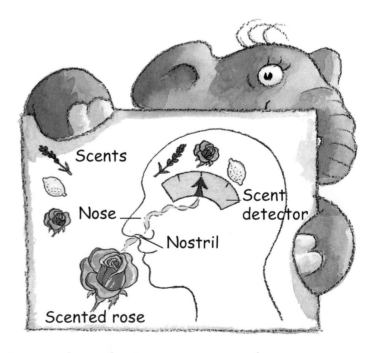

Scents

Scent detector

Nose

Nostril

Scented rose

As you breathe in, scents travel up your nose. Each scent has particles of a different size and shape. Scent detectors in your nose can tell the difference between them.

See for yourself! ✋

1 Put a little water in two saucers. Stand one on top of a radiator or a sunny windowsill. Stand the other on a plate of ice in a shadier area.

Water

Ice

Water

Good scents!

WOW!

Mmm!

2 Ask a grown-up to help you add a few drops of scented oil, such as lavender, to each saucer and wait a little while.

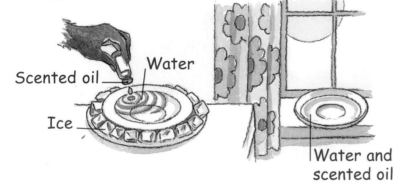

Scented oil

Water

Ice

Water and scented oil

Smells can have an effect on our brains, although we may not notice. Some scents, such as lavender and camomile, help us to relax. Others, including lemon and tea tree help us to be more wide awake.

3 Then walk around sniffing. Which one starts to smell first? Which smells stronger? Warmth should help the smells escape into the air.

Water and scented oil

Escaping vapour

Be careful with essential oils – they are very strong.

19

What lives in my bedroom?

What did one bedbug say to the other?

Fancy a bite?

Some creepy-crawlies find your bedroom just as cosy as you do. Spiders walk easily up walls and drainpipes. Climbing plants and window boxes help them to find their way in. At night, moths, May-bugs and daddy-long-legs (craneflies) fly in through open windows, attracted by the light. Most of these small visitors are harmless, but biting fleas (which hitch a ride on pets), and mosquitoes, are out looking for blood. In autumn, ladybirds and butterflies may arrive, looking for somewhere to *hibernate*.

What is an insect?

May-bugs, moths and butterflies are flying insects. They have six legs and large feelers called antennae. Fleas are insects too, but they don't have wings.

Spiders and mites are not insects, they are *arachnids*. They cannot fly and have eight legs. Slugs and snails have soft bodies and no legs at all. They are called *molluscs*.

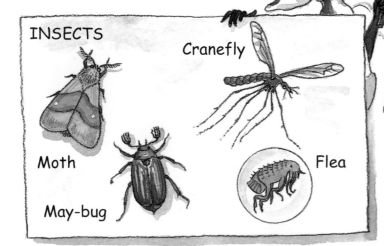

INSECTS

Cranefly

Moth

May-bug

Flea

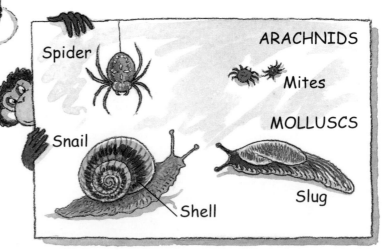

ARACHNIDS

Spider

Mites

MOLLUSCS

Snail

Shell

Slug

See for yourself! ✋

1 What can you hear when it is quiet at night? You might hear the buzz of a fly or the whine of a mosquito.

Mosquito

2 In winter, have a peep in the folds of your curtains. You may find a sleeping ladybird or butterfly. Do not disturb it. It will wake up and fly away in spring.

Butterfly

Ladybird

3 Look out for the slimy trails of slugs and snails which have wandered indoors during the night.

Snail

Snail trail

Sneezy bugs

WOW!

Achooo!

The tiniest uninvited guests are house dust mites which live in dust. They feed on mould growing on anything slightly damp, including your bedding. People can sometimes be allergic to them. They can make us sneeze and wheeze.

House dust mite

Don't touch bugs that bite or sting!

Why do I draw the curtains?

It is easier to sleep in the dark, because while your eyes are open they are keeping your brain busy by sending it messages. When you close your eyes to go to sleep, there is nothing to look at and you aren't tempted to open them again. Modern houses have big windows made of colourless glass that let in lots of light. By covering them with curtains or blinds, you can keep out the light while you are sleeping. You will not be disturbed by streetlights, moonlight, the headlights of passing cars, or by the Sun when it rises in the morning.

Why do you need a pencil?

To draw the curtains!

Light and materials

Something which is *transparent* lets light through it. You can see what is on the other side. Opaque materials hold back all the light. You can't see through them at all.

Light can't go through blindfolds.

Light can go through glasses.

Not all glass is colourless. Some glass can let through only one colour, some is dark, and some looks milky or pearly.

Dark glass

Coloured glass

Pearly glass

See for yourself!

1 Find a nice, bright sunbeam or shine a desk lamp onto a wall. The light shining on the wall has travelled through air, which is transparent and colourless.

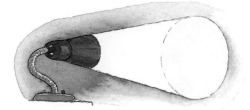

2 Look through a clear piece of plastic or clingfilm. You can see what is on the other side because it is transparent. Hold it in the light beam. There is almost no shadow.

Light shadow of edge

3 Hold a thick piece of card up to the light. You can't see anything through it, because it is opaque. Hold it in the light beam. It casts a dark shadow.

Dark shadow

4 Use other objects, such as drinking glasses, sweet wrappers and coloured plastic. How much light goes through them? What kind of light can you see?

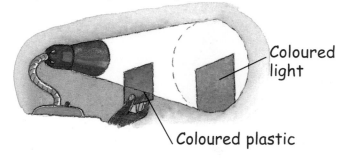

Coloured light

Coloured plastic

What's cooking?

WOW!

Several thousand years ago, someone heated a mixture of sand, ashes and limestone until it was red-hot and runny. They had discovered the recipe for glass!

Hot furnace

Sand

Lime

Ash

Glass

Always handle glass very carefully.

23

Why can night seem scary?

What's a ghost's favourite game?

Hide and shriek!

Have strange night-time noises ever made you shiver? Don't worry – there is an explanation! Sounds made when something moves reach us as vibrations in the air. Busy daytime noises stop at night, but it is not totally silent. We often hear noises that are harder to hear clearly during the day, such as noises made by the house itself or sounds made by night-time animals. If we hear a strange sound, or see a shadowy shape in the dark, we try to imagine what it is, but we don't always get it right!

Spooky sounds

Floorboards and stairs that get longer (expand) in the heat of the day, get shorter (contract) as they cool down. They creak as they move.

Sound travels further at night. A layer of warm air above the cold night air reflects sound like a mirror reflects light.

Owls hoot

Mice squeak

Wood creaks as it moves.

Air still warm from the day

Reflected sound

Dogs bark

Cats meow

Air near the ground cools when the Sun sets.

See for yourself!

1 Can you make your own spooky night-time noises? Try howling like a dog or hooting like an owl.

Ooooo!

Tu-whit Tu-whoo!

2 See what creepy, creaky noises you can make by bending things or rubbing things together. Think how you might do the sound effects for a play about a haunted house.

Crunch!

Twang!

3 Some things can look scary in the dark. Does anything in your room, like a dressing-gown, make a spooky shape?

Super-hearing!

WOW!

Bats make high-pitched squeaks.

Children have more sensitive ears than adults, and often hear higher sounds. They can sometimes even pick up the *ultrasonic* sounds made by bats. So it is not surprising they hear strange noises!

There's no need to be afraid of the dark.

How does a cradle rock?

When a cradle stands still on its rockers, it is *balanced* – we say it is in *equilibrium*. If you give the cradle a push from one side, this acts as a *force* that upsets the equilibrium. The cradle tries to rock back to its starting position, but it moves too fast, and goes too far in the opposite direction. Each rock becomes smaller than the last, so the cradle slows down, and finally comes to rest where it started. To keep the cradle rocking, you must give it another push as it slows down.

> What is the centre of gravity?

> The letter V!

Keeping a balance

When the cradle is still, it is balanced. *Gravity* pulls down on one side as much as it does on the other.

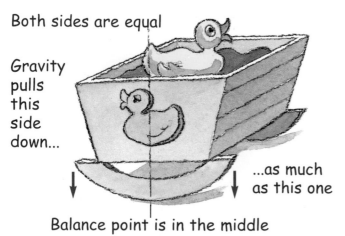

Both sides are equal

Gravity pulls this side down...

...as much as this one

Balance point is in the middle

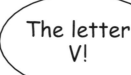

Old balance point

New balance point

When it is pushed out of position, there is more of the cradle on one side of the balance point than the other.

As the cradle rocks, it moves backwards and forwards until both sides are balanced again.

See for yourself! 🖐

1 To make rockers, cut out a circle the size of a saucer from a piece of card. Cut this in half and trim off the corners.

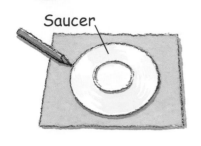
Saucer

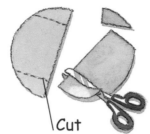
Cut

2 To make your cradle, tape or glue a rocker to each end of a large matchbox or a small tea packet.

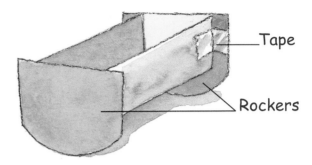
Tape

Rockers

3 Hang a small button on a thread down the middle of one rocker. Make a mark on the card halfway down, under the thread.

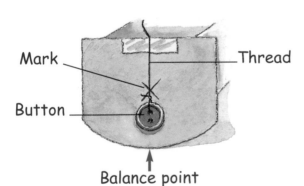
Mark

Thread

Button

Balance point

4 Tilt your cradle. On which side of the thread is the mark? When you let go, it will always rock in the direction of the mark.

Cradle rocks back this way

Cradle rocks back this way

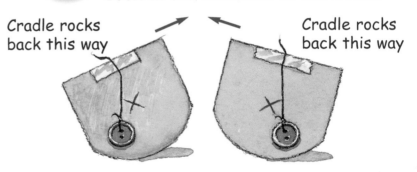

Going green!

Gentle rocking can help you fall asleep. However, too much rocking can make you feel queasy. It upsets the part of your inner ear that helps you keep your balance.

WOW!

Some animals like swinging too!

What is moonlight?

The Sun gives out energy in the form of heat and light which travel through space. Some of it reaches the Earth to give us bright, hot sunshine, but some of it hits the Moon before bouncing to the Earth. This reflected sunlight is called moonlight. Because the Moon's light has to travel further than the Sun's before reaching us, it is dimmer and cooler than sunlight. As the Moon moves around the Earth, the amount of reflected light that we see changes.

Why isn't the Moon hungry?

Because it's full!

The changing light of the Moon

FULL MOON

Earth

Night Day

Moon

Sun

Full Moon shines on dark side of the Earth.

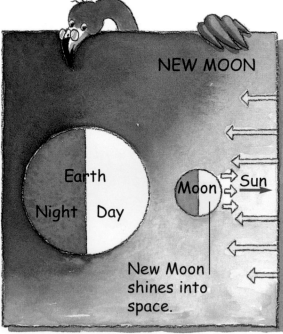

NEW MOON

Earth

Night Day

Moon Sun

New Moon shines into space.

There is most moonlight at Full Moon, when we see the Moon as a complete circle. When the Moon is in the wrong position to reflect light back to Earth, we see only part of it. When there is a New Moon, we get no reflected light at all, and we can't see the Moon from Earth at night.

28

See for yourself!

1 Put a ball in the top of a mug. This is the 'Earth'. Fix a sticker on the side and shine a lamp at it. This is the 'Sun' shining on you (the sticker) during the day.

This side is in shadow. It is night on this side.

Earth — You — Sun

2 Turn the 'Earth' around until the sticker is at the edge of the shadow. This is sunset. Now turn it until you are in night-time.

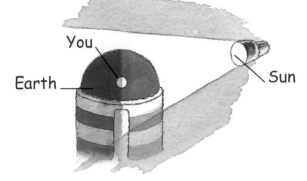

You — Earth — Sun

3 Tape a shiny silver coin, or ball, to the end of a pencil. Hold it behind the 'Earth', so that it reflects the 'Sun's' light on to the sticker. This is a Full Moon.

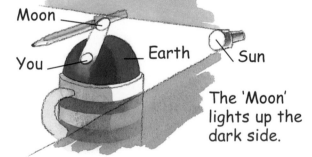

Moon — You — Earth — Sun

The 'Moon' lights up the dark side.

4 Move the 'Moon' around and try to reflect light on to the sticker. You will find that no other position gives out so much 'moonlight'.

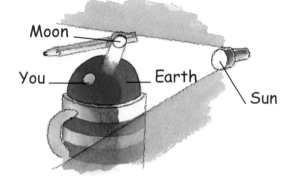

Moon — You — Earth — Sun

Earthshine

WOW!

If you were on the Moon, you would see light reflected from the Earth – 'earthshine'. When we have a New Moon, the Moon has a 'Full Earth' and, when we have a Full Moon, the Moon has a 'New Earth'.

Look out for a moon-shadow!

29

Bedroom quiz

1 How does your duvet keep you warm?
    a) It traps cold air
    b) It traps warm air
    c) It traps sunlight

2 What makes a 'clockwork' clock keep time?
    a) Candles
    b) Sand
    c) Gearwheels

3 What sometimes happens to your hair when you brush it?
    a) It stands on end
    b) It changes colour
    c) It stops growing

4 What makes a light bulb give out light?
    a) Gravity
    b) Energy
    c) Friction

5 What type of animal does wool come from?
    a) A cow
    b) A horse
    c) A sheep

6 What kind of creature is a butterfly?
    a) An insect
    b) An arachnid
    c) A mollusc

7 Where are your scent detectors?
    a) In your nose
    b) In your ears
    c) In your throat

8 What type of material is glass?
    a) Transparent
    b) Stretchy
    c) Spongy

9 How do sounds reach us through the air?
    a) As vibrations
    b) As light rays
    c) As shadows

10 What makes the light reflected by the Moon?
    a) The stars
    b) The Sun
    c) The Earth

Answers on page 32

Glossary

Arachnids
Small, wingless animals with bodies that are in two sections, and eight jointed legs.

Balanced
When forces that could cause movement in one direction are cancelled out by forces in the opposite direction.

Convection
Movement of heat through a liquid or gas, carried by currents of heated particles.

Digital
Showing an amount or time as a series of digits, or numbers, for example on a digital clock.

Dyes
Substances that stick to cloth fibres and colour them.

Electrically charged
When a surface that is electrically charged has too many or too few electrons.

Electricity
A type of energy carried along by electrically charged particles.

Electrons
Tiny particles that carry electrical energy.

Energy
The ability to do work or action.

Equilibrium
A state in which things are balanced.

Essential oils
Perfumed, oily substances produced by some plants.

Evaporate
To change from a visible liquid into an invisible vapour, without being hot enough to boil.

Fibres
Long, thin, flexible thread-like structures.

Filament
The thin, metal wire in a light bulb, which can get white-hot without melting.

Force
A push or pull which changes something's movement or shape.

Gravity
Earth's downward pull, which makes things fall.

Heat
A type of energy that warms things up, making them expand, evaporate, melt or boil.

Hibernate
To spend the winter in a deep sleep to avoid the cold and lack of food.

Insulation
Material used to slow down or stop the movement of heat.

Light
The energy given out by white-hot objects that lets us see things.

Liquid crystal display
An electronic display of numbers and letters, made of liquid crystals between two sheets of glass or plastic.

Molluscs
Animals with no backbone, and bodies made of muscle, some of which have shells.

Opaque
When something does not allow light to pass through it.

Particles
Very small parts or pieces of something.

Poles
The two ends of a magnet. When the magnet is free to move, the ends point towards Earth's North and South Poles.

Reflect
To bounce light, heat or sound off a surface.

Senses
Parts of the nervous system (the network of cells that takes messages around the body) that tell the body what is happening to it.

Static electricity
Electrical energy that stays in one place, instead of flowing as a current.

Synthetic
Man-made, not natural.

Transparent
Something that you can see through.

Ultrasonic
Vibrations which are often too fast for the human ear to detect as sound.

Vacuum
A space from which the air has been taken out.

Vibrate
To move back and forth quickly.

White-hot
When something gets so hot that it can't keep all its energy in, it gives out white light as well as heat.

Index

Answers to Bedroom quiz on page 30
1 It traps warm air. 2 Gearwheels.
3 It stands on end. 4 Energy. 5 A sheep.
6 An insect. 7 In your nose. 8 Transparent.
9 As vibrations. 10 The Sun.